Ending the Struggle

Manage ADHD through Better Communication

Table of Contents

1. Introduction ... 1

2. Understanding ADHD: A Comprehensive Overview ... 2

    2.1. The Nature of ADHD ... 2

    2.2. Symptoms and Types of ADHD ... 2

    2.3. Factors Contributor to ADHD ... 3

    2.4. Diagnosing ADHD ... 4

    2.5. Treatment of ADHD ... 4

    2.6. Living with ADHD ... 5

    2.7. Wrapping up ... 5

3. The Power of Communication: An Introduction ... 6

    3.1. Active Listening and Empathy ... 6

    3.2. Non-Verbal Communication and ADHD ... 7

    3.3. Encouraging Expression and Providing Constructive Feedback ... 7

    3.4. Cultivating a Safe Communication Environment ... 8

    3.5. Progressing Towards Open, Positive communication ... 8

4. ADHD and Social Interactions: Challenges and Potential ... 10

    4.1. Impulsivity and its Impact ... 10

    4.2. Inattention: A Double-Edged Sword ... 10

    4.3. Communication Issues and the Potential for Growth ... 11

    4.4. Tips for Improving Social Interactions ... 11

    4.5. Summarizing the Journey ... 12

5. Communication Styles and ADHD: Finding the Right Fit ... 13

    5.1. Understanding Communication Styles ... 13

    5.2. The Interplay of ADHD and Communication Styles ... 14

    5.3. Assertive Communication: A Key to Managing ADHD ... 14

    5.4. Strategizing for Successful Communication: Techniques and Tools ... 15

5.5. Tailoring Communication in Relationships 16

6. Listening Skills: Key to Empathetic Communication 17

6.1. The Importance of Listening in Communication 17

6.2. The Art of Active Listening 18

6.3. The Power of Empathetic Listening 18

6.4. Active and Empathetic Listening: A Lifelong Skill 20

7. Strategies for Clear, Direct Communication with ADHD 21

7.1. Understanding ADHD and Communication Variances 21

7.2. Active Listening 21

7.3. Clarity and Brevity 22

7.4. Non-Verbal Communication 22

7.5. Understand and Adjust to Communication Styles 23

8. The Impact of Non-Verbal Communication 25

8.1. Non-Verbal Communication: The Unspoken Language 25

8.2. Decoding The ADHD Non-Verbal Signals 26

8.3. The ADHF and Body Language Disconnect 26

8.4. The Power Of Facial Expressions 27

8.5. Tone Of Voice: An Often Overlooked Aspect 27

8.6. Timing And Spacing: The Silent Factors 27

9. Improving Communication: Tools and Techniques 29

9.1. Understanding ADHD and Its Impact on Communication ... 29

9.2. Mindful Dialogue 29

9.3. Leveraging Technology 30

9.4. Visual Aids 30

9.5. Improving Body Language 30

9.6. The Power of Pause 30

9.7. Positive Affirmations 30

9.8. Social Storytelling 31

9.9. Role-Play 31

9.10. Communication skills training 31

10. Case Studies: Successful Change through Better Conversation . . 32

    10.1. Case Study 1: Improving Parent-Child Relationship 32

    10.2. Case Study 2: Improving Spousal Relationship 33

    10.3. Case Study 3: Enhancing Teacher-Student Interactions 33

    10.4. Case Study 4: Enhancing Professional Relationships 34

    10.5. Case Study 5: Self-Understanding and Self-Regulation 34

11. Looking Forward: Creating a Positive Communication
Environment 36

    11.1. The Art of Active Listening 36

    11.2. Importance of Empathy 36

    11.3. Constructive Feedback and ADHD 37

    11.4. Creating a Safe Space for Open Dialogue 37

    11.5. Encouraging Self-Expression 38

    11.6. Emphasizing on Patience and Persistence 38

Chapter 1. Introduction

Welcome to a transformative journey that can drastically enhance the lives of individuals managing ADHD and those around them! Our special report, "Ending the Struggle: Manage ADHD through Better Communication," is a lively, accessible and engaging resource full of practical advice, research-based strategies, and illuminating anecdotes. Unearthing the power of better communication, this guide brings a groundbreaking perspective to manage ADHD, aiming to reduce conflict, foster empathy and most importantly, alleviate struggle. The techniques discussed inside are not merely theoretical posts but well-tested and proven methods that have already reshaped countless lives. This report's empowering and optimistic language is designed to inspire hope and incite positive change. So why wait? Step into a world filled with understanding and growth, and harness the power of effective communication to manage ADHD like never before. Purchasing this special report might just be the best decision you'll make today for a brighter, more harmonious tomorrow.

Chapter 2. Understanding ADHD: A Comprehensive Overview

The human brain, a powerful orchestra of billions of neurons, balances different thoughts, emotions, and actions in harmony. When this balance is disrupted, a behavioral condition develops known as Attention Deficit Hyperactivity Disorder, or ADHD. This condition is typically diagnosed in childhood but can persist into adulthood, characterized by symptoms such as inattention, hyperactivity, and impulsivity. The following sections delve into a broad overview of ADHD, aiming to foster enhanced understanding and encourage empathetic interaction.

2.1. The Nature of ADHD

ADHD is fundamentally a neurobiological disorder, not a consequence of poor parenting, lack of discipline, or low intelligence. Groundbreaking research has found that ADHD is linked with certain irregularities in how different parts of the brain communicate with each other, and sometimes, even their size.

The prefrontal cortex, the area responsible for executive functions like attention, response inhibition, and regulating behavior, tends to be smaller and less active in people with ADHD. These individuals may, therefore, struggle with activities that involve planning, focusing, remembering instructions, and juggling multiple tasks at once.

2.2. Symptoms and Types of ADHD

ADHD is not a one-size-fits-all diagnosis, and it presents with different symptoms in different individuals. Broadly, the symptoms fall into two categories: inattentiveness and hyperactivity/impulsivity.

Inattentiveness is characterized by - being easily distracted, forgetfulness, making careless mistakes, difficulty organizing tasks, persistently losing items, and difficulty in sustaining attention in tasks or play.

Hyperactivity and Impulsivity are marked by - an urge to move constantly, excessive talking, difficulty waiting one's turn, frequently interrupting others, and acting without thinking.

Decades of research have classified ADHD into three types - primarily inattentive, primarily hyperactive/impulsive, and combined type.

2.3. Factors Contributor to ADHD

ADHD does not have a singular cause, rather it arises from a combination of various genetic, environmental, and neurological factors. Studies of twins indicate a significant genetic component, with ADHD often running in families. Certain environmental influences, such as smoking or alcohol use during pregnancy, premature birth, and low birth weight, are linked to a higher risk of developing ADHD.

While there's no evidence linking diet or sugar consumption to ADHD, some studies suggest certain food additives or high levels of processed sugar might exacerbate symptoms in some people.

It's essential also to understand that ADHD is not caused by excessive screen time, sugar, or poor parenting.

2.4. Diagnosing ADHD

Diagnosis of ADHD is multi-layered, involving clinical interviews, medical examinations, and behavior rating scales. Because many conditions can mimic the symptoms of ADHD, thorough diagnostic testing is essential to rule out conditions like depression, anxiety, and certain types of learning disabilities.

Unfortunately, there is no single definitive test for ADHD, and the process of diagnosing can be a journey in itself, with a comprehensive evaluation needing to be conducted by a qualified health professional.

2.5. Treatment of ADHD

The journey of managing ADHD generally involves a combination approach - behavioral therapy, medication, effective communication, and a healthy lifestyle. Stimulant and non-stimulant medications affect brain chemicals in a way that helps reduce ADHD symptoms and improve functioning.

Accompanying medication with behavioral therapy can have even more profound effects. Cognitive-behavioral therapy (CBT) works by changing negative patterns of thinking and behavior. It's particularly effective for adults with ADHD, who may benefit enormously from learning organizational strategies and social interaction techniques.

No matter what treatment is chosen, it's essential to remember that ADHD is manageable. With understanding, empathy, open communication, and a willingness to work collaboratively, managing ADHD can become less of a struggle over time, and more of a journey of growth.

2.6. Living with ADHD

Living with or managing someone with ADHD can be challenging. It's important therefore to seek support from professionals and peer groups. Establishing a routine, getting proper nutrition, regular exercise, enough sleep, and instituting a positive reinforcing behavior system can greatly assist.

Finally, understanding is the first step to accept ADHD. Remember, having ADHD is not a moral failing or a character flaw. It merely means that the individual's brain works a little differently. By recognizing this, we set the stage for better communication, empathy, and a more harmonious life.

2.7. Wrapping up

ADHD is a complex disorder that has a profound impact on an individual's life. Despite the challenges, people with ADHD possess unique strengths, such as creativity, resilience, and a unique way of looking at the world. Understanding ADHD, therefore, is not just about understanding the difficulties, but about delineating the strengths and fostering them for a more fulfilled and accomplished life. Reach out for professional help if you or a loved one exhibits signs. Remember, an ADHD diagnosis is not the end, but the beginning of a journey, with knowledge, acceptance, therapeutic intervention, and a dash of positive perspective forming the roadmap to managing this condition.

Chapter 3. The Power of Communication: An Introduction

In its simplest form, communication can be defined as the exchange of ideas, messages, or information between two or more people. This involves a sender transmitting an idea, which is then processed and understood by a receiver. However, managing ADHD is no simple task, and therefore necessitates more nuanced forms of communication. More than just exchanging words, effective communication in the context of ADHD management embodies a range of strategies including active listening, interpreting non-verbal cues, providing constructive feedback, and empathetic understanding of the person with ADHD.

3.1. Active Listening and Empathy

Fundamental to improved communication and ADHD management is the practice of active listening, an essential tool in understanding the unique experiences and perspectives of those with ADHD. Often, individuals with ADHD feel misunderstood. Their minds racing at a pace that others may find difficult to keep up with, and their thoughts, frequently jumping in various directions, may seem confusing to someone unaccustomed to the ADHD thought process.

Active listening involves more than just hearing what the person says. It requires deliberate focus, concentration, and a genuine desire to understand. Nodding in agreement, paraphrasing, summarizing, or asking clarifying questions are all indicative of this crucial skill. In doing so, individuals with ADHD not only feel heard but are also empowered to express their thoughts and feelings more freely.

Empathy goes hand in hand with active listening. By placing yourself in the shoes of the person with ADHD, you're embracing their perspective. This is immensely reassuring for them.

3.2. Non-Verbal Communication and ADHD

Encompassing body language, facial expressions, and tone of voice, non-verbal cues are a crucial part of communication. For individuals with ADHD, these messages can be more prominent and expressive than the spoken words. Understanding and interpreting non-verbal cues are vital in ensuring effective communication. The occasional distraction or a perceived lack of focus may sometimes camouflage the true feelings of individuals with ADHD, often expressed more vividly through their non-verbal cues.

Equally important is our ability to regulate our non-verbal communication when interacting with people managing ADHD. The manner of our body language, tone of our voice, or the expressions on our face may convey messages that we may not have intended, or amplify the ones we did.

3.3. Encouraging Expression and Providing Constructive Feedback

It can be challenging for those with ADHD to match the pace of their thoughts with that of their speech. Often, they may blurt details abruptly, losing the cohesiveness of their narration or their line of argument. Encouraging their forms of expression can be a significant step in making communication more effective. For all their hyperspeed thinking, people diagnosed with ADHD can be uniquely imaginative and creative. Harnessing this potential requires patience, open minds, and consequently, refined ways of interaction.

Constructive feedback is a two-part process - genuinely praising the person's efforts and offering perspective on the areas that need improvement. The feedback loop, when used effectively, can motivate the person with ADHD, making them feel appreciated and valued.

3.4. Cultivating a Safe Communication Environment

A supportive environment makes a world of difference in effective communication. By encouraging open dialogues, a safe communication environment allows individuals with ADHD to express themselves freely without fear of judgment or reprimands. This can stimulate their creativity, encourage them to share their ideas, and facilitate their integration into social or classroom settings.

3.5. Progressing Towards Open, Positive communication

Whether it's at home, work, school, or a social gathering, open communication plays a crucial role. It's about engaging in discussions, asking questions, seeking clarifications, or expressing opinions freely and respectfully. Tasks and expectations can be laid out clearly, making it easier for those managing ADHD.

Positive communication is also key to cultivating supportive relationships with individuals who have ADHD. This involves focusing on strengths, celebrating the wins, however small, and nurturing an atmosphere of acceptance and understanding.

In conclusion, communication is a potent tool in managing ADHD. By honing our communication strategies and skills - active listening, empathy, understanding non-verbal cues, providing constructive feedback, crafting safe communication environments, and promoting open, positive communication - we can significantly improve the quality of life for individuals with ADHD and those interacting with them. As we delve further into this guide, specific strategies and tools will be shared to make these processes more tangible and implementable.

Chapter 4. ADHD and Social Interactions: Challenges and Potential

Those living with ADHD often encounter unique obstacles when it comes to social interactions, due to challenges such as impulsivity, inattention, and even communication issues. Such challenges, however, needn't be perceived solely as impediments. In fact, there is a vast reservoir of potential that lies untapped in these interactions. This section delves into the various challenges associated with ADHD in the arena of social exchanges and explores how these very obstacles can serve as springboards towards greater understanding and growth.

4.1. Impulsivity and its Impact

Persons with ADHD often exhibit impulsivity, a trait characterized by spur-of-the-moment actions or responses. This impulsivity could manifest in numerous ways, such as interrupting others, hyperactive behavior, or making decisions without thoroughly considering the consequences. These behaviors can inadvertently place a strain on the person's social relationships. On the flip side, impulsivity can also yield positive outcomes, as it often encourages creativity and spontaneity, promoting lively, engaging interactions.

4.2. Inattention: A Double-Edged Sword

Individuals diagnosed with ADHD might have difficulty maintaining attention during social interactions. They may become distracted or find it strenuous to stay focused on the conversation at hand. This could potentially make their companions feel unseen, unheard, or misunderstood. However, afflicted individuals can tap into the potential of this challenge by developing techniques to channel their wandering minds towards creative ideation and problem-solving, making them inspiring thinkers and innovators.

4.3. Communication Issues and the Potential for Growth

Communication skills are vitally important in social scenarios, but individuals with ADHD may sometimes struggle with effective conversation management. From having difficulty following a conversation thread to inadvertently overlooking social cues, such issues may cause misunderstanding, leading to possible social friction.

However, these communication challenges can also lead to personal growth. By striving to enhance these skills, individuals with ADHD can learn to better understand their strengths and weaknesses, developing empathy and becoming more introspective along the way. The undertaking to improve will not only benefit their social life but also their overall self-awareness, positively impacting every aspect of their lives.

4.4. Tips for Improving Social Interactions

Despite the challenges, it is entirely possible for those with ADHD to have successful, meaningful social interactions. Here are a few tips built on empathy and understanding:

1. Educate Yourself and Others: Understanding how ADHD affects you personally can enlighten your social circle, helping them see past the setbacks to the person you are.

2. Implement Communication Techniques: Learn how to manage conversations better. This could mean utilizing active listening or honing strategies to stay focused during a discussion.

3. Understand Social Cues: Watch for social signals from your companions to help modulate your behavior or response as required.

By taking up these strategies, individuals with ADHD can transform social interactions from anxiety-ridden occurrences to empowering dialogues, enlarging their emotional toolset and fostering profound connections.

4.5. Summarizing the Journey

Combating the challenges of social interactions requires leveraging the potential residing beneath each issue. By transforming perceived weaknesses into learning opportunities, individuals with ADHD can enhance not just their social lives but their overall sense of self-worth and mastery. Manifesting this transformation is reliant on an amalgamation of self-understanding, effective communication techniques, and an active endeavor to recognize and understand social cues.

Approached from this perspective, ADHD ceases to be a mere condition requiring management; instead, it becomes a part of a broader journey towards personal growth and robust social connections. The real potential, therefore, lies not just in the management of challenges but also in empowering ourselves to use these challenges as stepping stones to a more fulfilled, socially integrated existence.

Chapter 5. Communication Styles and ADHD: Finding the Right Fit

Understanding different communication styles and how they intersect with ADHD symptoms is significant in improving the dialogue between individuals with ADHD and those around them. Both in personal and professional spheres, communication styles play an essential role. People with ADHD often develop unique patterns of communication, primarily based on their way of processing information. Therefore, recognizing one's personal communication style as well as the need to adapt to others is crucial.

5.1. Understanding Communication Styles

Four fundamental communication styles are generally recognized: passive, aggressive, passive-aggressive, and assertive. People with ADHD often fluctuate between these styles, depending on the situation, mood, and people involved.

Passive communication often includes avoiding conflict, not speaking up for oneself, and withholding one's feelings and needs. Conversely, aggressive communication can lead to confrontations, speaking over others, and often defending oneself hastily. As for passive-aggressive communication, it covertly combines both passive and aggressive styles, where the communicator expresses discontent indirectly. Lastly, assertive communication asserts one's rights without disrespecting others and is considered the most balanced and effective communication style.

ADHD symptoms often get intermingled with these communication styles. Hyperfocus might morph into passionate debates leading to aggressive communication. Similarly, attention-switching difficulties could lead to misunderstandings fostering passive communication. By identifying these styles and their interplay with ADHD, we can consciously choose more effective ways to communicate.

5.2. The Interplay of ADHD and Communication Styles

ADHD typically influences inattention, impulsivity, and hyperactivity - three parameters dramatically affecting communication styles. People with ADHD might find it hard to maintain attention during conversations, leading to misunderstandings or feelings of disrespect. Impulsivity can result in not fully thinking through responses, causing regret later. Hyperactivity might manifest as an overabundance of ideas and thoughts, which might seem overwhelming to others.

Understanding these ADHD symptoms and their influence on communication is invaluable in developing effective communication strategies. Awareness of one's patterns provides a stepping stone towards forging better communication styles.

5.3. Assertive Communication: A Key to Managing ADHD

Assertiveness is a useful skill for those with ADHD. It values open, honest, and direct communication without comparisons to others. With practice, this healthy and balanced style can reduce misunderstandings and foster more positive interpersonal relationships.

Practicing assertive communication involves clearly expressing your thoughts, needs, and feelings, showing understanding towards others, and standing up for your rights respectfully. For those with ADHD, incorporating this communication style involves work but offers numerous benefits.

5.4. Strategizing for Successful Communication: Techniques and Tools

Here are some strategies specially tailored for individuals negotiating with ADHD to embrace an assertive communication style.

1. Slow Down and Listen: By consciously slowing down their thought process and focusing on the conversation at hand, ADHD individuals can better process information, leading to more precise responses.

2. Embrace Empathy: Understanding another person's perspective can greatly enhance communication. Empathy helps in formulating respectful and considerate responses.

3. Use 'I' statements: Constructing sentences around 'I' rather than 'you' can be instrumental in avoiding blame and promoting better mutual understanding.

4. Non-Verbal Communication: Emphasizing non-verbal cues like body language and facial expressions can further reinforce the message that one is trying to convey.

5. Preparation and Practice: Just like any other skill, effective communication takes preparation and practice. Scheduled, deliberate practice using these strategies can make a significant positive difference over time.

5.5. Tailoring Communication in Relationships

For ADHD individuals, improving communication is not only key in professional settings but also within personal relationships. The ability to express oneself confidently and openly strengthens bonds between partners, family, and friends.

In relationships, understanding each other's communication style can bridge gaps and increase satisfaction. By honestly articulating needs and emotions, conflicts can decrease while empathy, understanding, and harmony multiply. Also, it's worth understanding that timing, attention to the presence of others, and making adjustments based on the listener's needs can further smooth communication.

In conclusion, exploring communication styles and their influences is elemental to managing ADHD. Embracing assertiveness, understanding other's perspectives, and taking small steps towards change can incrementally and substantially enhance communication, impacting all areas of life positively. Remember, the power of effective communication is not to win an argument but to ensure understanding, create clarity, and foster growth in relationships. By harnessing these strategies, individuals with ADHD can benefit enormously, bettering both their lives and others around them.

Chapter 6. Listening Skills: Key to Empathetic Communication

In a world that never stops talking, truly listening to someone can be the most valuable gift you can offer.

Let's start by stating a sobering fact. Communication is not simply about talking. It's a two-way process: speaking and listening. For individuals with ADHD, developing effective listening skills is particularly essential since it can evoke empathy and understanding, thereby making their interaction more cohesive, enriching and less fraught with conflicts.

6.1. The Importance of Listening in Communication

Effective listening is a coveted skill. Not only does it enable us to understand and learn from others, but also improves the quality of our relationships by making others feel heard and valued. Listening is particularly vital in communicating with individuals with ADHD. Through effective listening, we can get a better understanding of their experiences, build empathy and ultimately, provide them with the support they require.

Moreover, by being a good listener, there can be a considerable reduction in the misunderstandings and conflicts that can be commonplace for those grappling with ADHD. Misunderstandings often crop up when either party lacks the ability to actively listen. This simple yet potent tool paves the way for clear, open, and fruitful conversations among individuals managing ADHD and those around them.

6.2. The Art of Active Listening

Active listening involves full engagement in the conversation—both verbally and non-verbally. It requires giving undivided attention to the speaker, comprehending their message, giving appropriate feedback, and not interrupting. It might sound easy, but it requires awareness and practice.

Here are some of the actions associated with active listening:

1. **Pay Full Attention:** To actively listen, eliminate distractions and give your full attention to the speaker. For individuals with ADHD, this might prove to be difficult, and so it might be helpful to find a quiet place to communicate.

2. **Get the Complete Message:** Make a conscious effort to understand the entire message, from facts to feelings, rather than hastily forming a response in your mind.

3. **Give Visual Feedback:** If you're in a face-to-face conversation, employ body language to show engagement by making eye contact or nodding.

4. **Interject Sensitively:** Only interject if it's necessary to gain clarification and always do so in a sensitive and respectful way.

5. **Reflect on What's Been Said:** After the speaker has finished talking, take a moment to process. Reflect before replying, allowing the speaker's message to truly sink in.

6.3. The Power of Empathetic Listening

Emphatic listening moves beyond simply understanding the words or the message of the speaker. It's about attaining a deeper comprehension of their feelings and emotions. It involves "stepping into their shoes" and viewing the world from their perspective. This ultimately fosters empathy, a crucial component needed in communication with those managing ADHD.

However, empathetic listening isn't something that comes naturally to most people. We often get consumed by our thoughts, experiences, and biases and might end up monopolizing conversations or trivializing the experiences of others.

The path to empathetic listening involves the following stages:

1. **Creating a Safe Environment:** For open and honest communication to happen, a safe zone needs to be created. This involves making the other person feel comfortable enough to freely share their ideas, without the fear of being ridiculed or invalidated. This is particularly crucial for individuals grappling with ADHD, who often struggle with self-expression.

2. **Understanding at an Emotional Level:** Empathetic listening involves understanding what the other person is feeling and why. It can be done by closely observing the emotional cues in their speech and body language. It's about going beyond the words uttered and delving into the ocean of underlying emotions.

3. **Displaying Empathy Through Your Response:** It's not enough to just understand the speaker's emotions. To fully demonstrate your comprehension of their feelings, your response has to be consciously imbued with empathy. Your words, tone, and body language must all reflect sincerity and compassion.

4. **Validating Their Feelings:** "I can understand why you might feel that way" is a powerful phrase. Validation reinforces their belief that their feelings are both authentic and important, which in turn boosts self-esteem.

6.4. Active and Empathetic Listening: A Lifelong Skill

Like any other essential life skills, active and empathetic listening are cultivated over time. Their importance and relevance are universal but they hold a magnified significance for individuals grappling with ADHD. Through practice and patience, you can become more comfortable with these skills. As a result, you'll be contributing to healthier and more harmonious future communication.

Remember, when interacting with individuals with ADHD, you're not just listening to words or understanding the vast world of their experiences; you're also creating an atmosphere of mutual respect, empathy, and understanding. The essence of communication lies not in speaking, but indeed in listening, and active and empathetic listening are the keys to unlock it.

Chapter 7. Strategies for Clear, Direct Communication with ADHD

Effective communication forms the bedrock of any relationship. For people with ADHD, clear, direct communication can significantly alleviate the problems associated with the disorder and foster stronger bonds among their interpersonal connections. Harnessing the power of effective communication can be tremendously beneficial and life-transforming.

7.1. Understanding ADHD and Communication Variances

Before delving deep into the communication strategies, it is of prime importance to understand how ADHD affects communication. ADHD influences the way people think, react, and process information. It can lead to challenges in maintaining attention, staying organized, and following through on tasks, which in turn can compromise effective communication.

People with ADHD often struggle with 'executive functions,' the range of mental skills that help us plan, focus attention, juggle multiple tasks, and manage time and space. This may make communication difficult, possibly leading to misunderstanding and conflict. Recognizing these potential communication challenges is an important first step towards devising measures to overcome them.

7.2. Active Listening

The first and perhaps the most important strategy for effective communication is active listening. Active listening involves not just hearing the words being spoken, but actively seeking to understand the complete message being relayed.

1. Paraphrasing: Paraphrasing is a crucial tool for active listening. By repeating back what you've heard in your own words, you're showing that you've understood the speaker's point of view.

2. Empathetic Responding: Empathetic responding is another vital aspect of active listening. Try to express understanding and empathy for feelings mentioned or implied by the speaker.

3. Open-Ended Questions: Engage the speaker by asking open-ended questions that promote discussion. This will foster a deeper understanding and connection.

7.3. Clarity and Brevity

Another essential strategy for effective communication, especially for individuals with ADHD, is to be clear and brief in conveying thoughts and instructions.

1. Be Explicit: Being explicit helps ensure that your message is received accurately. Say exactly what you mean, avoiding underlying hints or assumptions.

2. Use Short, Simple Sentences: People with ADHD often find it easier to grasp information broken down into short, simple sentences. Try to convey one thought per sentence.

3. Avoid Overloading Information: ADHD can make processing large amounts of information difficult. To avoid overwhelming the recipient, only share necessary and relevant information.

7.4. Non-Verbal Communication

Non-verbal communication is equally important when interacting with someone with ADHD.

1. Eye Contact: Eye contact is a powerful non-verbal communication tool which helps ensure that the person is engaged and is paying attention to what is being said.

2. Gestures: Simple gestures can help reinforce information. It not only aids in grabbing attention but also helps in better understanding and information retention.

3. Body Language: Body language speaks volumes. A relaxed and open posture suggests that you're receptive and approachable, which can help decrease any potential anxiety on the part of the ADHD individual.

7.5. Understand and Adjust to Communication Styles

Understanding and adjusting to different communication styles of individuals with ADHD is vital in crafting an effective communication strategy.

1. "In-the-Moment" Communicators: These individuals do well with impromptu, in-the-moment communication. For such individuals, spontaneous expressions of thoughts and feelings work better.

2. "Think-It-Over" Communicators: These individuals prefer having time to consider information before responding. Offering them this space can lead to more meaningful and effective communication.

3. "Action-Oriented" Communicators: These individuals prefer to work things out through action or movement. Participating in shared activities or engaging conversations while moving can greatly enhance communication with such individuals.

With the right techniques and strategies, communication with individuals managing ADHD can be significantly improved. It's important to practice these strategies consistently, as effective communication provides a foundation that can transform lives, foster empathy, and most importantly, reduce struggle.

Chapter 8. The Impact of Non-Verbal Communication

The human experience of interaction is a blend of language and a myriad of non-verbal cues, which are often instinctual and subconscious. Particularly in the context of ADHD, where verbal communication may at times become challenging, non-verbal communication takes on a crucial role. Non-verbal cues, which encompass facial expressions, body language, gestures, and even timing, can significantly impact both the sender and receiver of these messages. Therefore, understanding these unspoken languages is vital for successful communication and overall better management of ADHD.

8.1. Non-Verbal Communication: The Unspoken Language

Before we dive deeper, let's dwell on what non-verbal communication is and why it's of such critical importance. Non-verbal communication refers to all the communication not expressed in words. This includes body movements, voice inflection, facial expressions, eye contact, physical touch, and even the spacing and timing around a conversation. With ADHD, where verbal articulation may not always be effective, non-verbal cues can either break or seal the communication deal.

Now, let's go a step further and discuss the implications of non-verbal communication among those with ADHD.

8.2. Decoding The ADHD Non-Verbal Signals

A common trait among many individuals grappling with ADHD is the failure to accurately interpret non-verbal cues. For example, let's say during a conversation, an individual is speaking quickly, moving restlessly, or interrupting frequently. While these may be attributed to ADHD symptoms, to an uninformed observer, they might appear impatient, disinterested, or even disrespectful. It's essential to understand that the messages sent unintentionally through behavioral cues might contradict the verbal communication. Hence, correctly interpreting these signals can reduce misunderstandings and foster healthier interactions.

Awareness is the first step to change. So, understanding the nature and influence of non-verbal communication goes a long way in managing ADHD more effectively.

8.3. The ADHF and Body Language Disconnect

The ADHD and body language disconnect is another aspect of non-verbal communication that significantly impacts interpersonal relationships. Individuals with ADHD often struggle with maintaining appropriate physical space during conversation, are unaware of others' personal space, or may fidget excessively. This can be distracting or discomforting. Understanding and considering these aspects while interacting can help create a neutral and comfortable conversation atmosphere for everyone involved.

8.4. The Power Of Facial Expressions

Facial expressions carry strong emotional value and are key to deciphering someone's emotions. They can make the difference between a sympathetically understood conversation versus one perceived as hostile. However, the rapid-fire pace of emotional responses often associated with ADHD can present challenges. Training oneself or their dear ones with ADHD to have an increased awareness and control over their facial expressions can greatly enhance their communication skill set.

8.5. Tone Of Voice: An Often Overlooked Aspect

The tone of voice, loudness, speed, and intonation can provide clues to underlying emotions or thoughts during a conversation. It's common for individuals with ADHD to either talk excessively fast or extremely slow or have a louder-than-normal tone. Paying attention to these details can decode valuable non-verbal information, unveiling hidden emotions or thoughts.

8.6. Timing And Spacing: The Silent Factors

The importance of the timing and pace of conversations, the pauses, the silences, and the space maintained during interactions, often goes unnoticed. This silent aspect of non-verbal communication also broadly influences the overall dynamics of a conversation. With ADHD, people might unknowingly dominate the conversation, jump topics, or interrupt others. Being aware of these possibilities and actively monitoring these aspects can contribute significantly to effective communication.

To sum up, non-verbal communication impacts every aspect of interaction and relationship-building. For people with ADHD and those who interact with them, an understanding and mastery of this unspoken language is critical. It's not an overnight process, but the least we can do is be aware, patient, and consistently work towards enhancing these skills. As we journey through this process, we'll find ourselves and our relationships evolving, nuanced, and richer, contributing positively towards managing ADHD.

Chapter 9. Improving Communication: Tools and Techniques

Developing effective communication skills can prove to be a game-changer for individuals dealing with ADHD. This chapter explores an array of tools and techniques designed to improve the dimension of communication in people managing ADHD, to foster profound understanding and harmony in daily life.

9.1. Understanding ADHD and Its Impact on Communication

To improve communication, one must first understand how ADHD impacts it. Individuals with ADHD often struggle with filtering out extraneous information, becoming easily sidetracked. They may be overwhelmed by the process of organizing thoughts coherently, thus their messages may seem distracted and disjointed.

9.2. Mindful Dialogue

Incorporating principles of mindfulness in dialogues can greatly enhance communication.

Stay present: Active engagement in conversations, resisting the urge to let the mind wander, sustains the flow of effective communication. This can be achieved by mentally restating what the other person is saying and by maintaining eye contact.

Non-judgmental listening: Create a safe space where all voices are heard and respected. This encourages the open sharing of thoughts and ideas without fear of being criticized or dismissed.

9.3. Leveraging Technology

Modern technology offers several tools that can make communication less stressful for individuals with ADHD. Apps that manage time and tasks can help to stay organized. Speech-to-text apps can facilitate the smooth translation of spoken words into written text.

9.4. Visual Aids

Visual aids can greatly help individuals with ADHD in organizing and articulating thoughts. Mind maps, flowcharts, and diagrams can act as tools to visually represent and process information.

9.5. Improving Body Language

Non-verbal communication is often just as vital as the words spoken. Maintaining an open stance, making eye contact, and using gestures that align with the spoken message can send positive signals of engagement and understanding.

9.6. The Power of Pause

Pausing in conversations aids in processing information and in formulating a thoughtful response. Regular use of this technique can help individuals manage ADHD to reduce instances of impulsive speech and foster a more considered exchange of ideas.

9.7. Positive Affirmations

Using positive affirmations can replace self-deprecating thoughts and promote self-confidence, which improves communication.

9.8. Social Storytelling

This method involves narrating everyday scenarios and discussing appropriate responses. It helps in improving the ability to predict social cues and respond appropriately.

9.9. Role-Play

Role-play exercises immerse individuals in potential interpersonal encounters, thereby offering a safe space to practice and hone communication skills.

9.10. Communication skills training

Professional training or counseling can aid in learning communication skills, including speaking concisely, maintaining focus during conversations, and learning to interpret non-verbal cues.

By investing time in these tailored techniques, individuals challenged by ADHD can harness the power of effective communication and cultivate more meaningful and productive relationships. Remember, each person's journey through ADHD is unique, and it's essential to adapt these strategies to suit personal circumstances and challenges.

The most significant improvements often stem from persistence and patience, so incorporating these tools into daily life might take time and practice. However, the rewards - enhanced self-understanding, more precise expression, and improved relationships - are well worth the effort. Embrace the transformative power of effective communication and set the course for a life of greater understanding and harmony.

Chapter 10. Case Studies: Successful Change through Better Conversation

According to research, one of the most efficient ways to cope with ADHD is through better and more effective communication. Here we present a myriad of real-life scenarios that reinforce this belief. Presented as pseudo-anonymous narratives, these accounts were shared by individuals who directly confronted the turbulence created by ADHD and brought about remarkable improvements by employing enhanced communication strategies.

10.1. Case Study 1: Improving Parent-Child Relationship

Sophie, an 11 year-old girl, often experienced challenges in delivering her homework on time. Her mother, Laura, claimed that she found it difficult to make Sophie understand the importance of punctuality and discipline, leading to frequent arguments between them.

Laura sought assistance from a counselor, who suggested incorporating positive language in their conversation. As the idea was implemented, Sophie began to receive appreciation and encouragement rather than frustration and admonishment.

Giving positive acknowledgment started stimulating Sophie's willingness to fulfill her responsibilities. After a few weeks, Laura noticed a significant change in Sophie's behavior, improved concentration, and timely submission of homework.

10.2. Case Study 2: Improving Spousal Relationship

John and Emma, married for over a decade, were grappling with John's adult ADHD symptoms that were starting to strain their relationship. Emma found herself constantly reminding and nagging John about tasks, which led to resentment.

They decided to consult a therapist, who introduced them to open-ended communication. Rather than asking rhetorical or blaming questions, Emma started using open-ended conversation starters like "What do you think about...?" or "Could you help me understand...?" These structured dialogues provided John with comfortable space to express his thoughts and feelings.

Over time, this change in their communication style resulted in fewer conflicts and increased empathy. Both of them reported feeling more understood, suggesting the power of appropriate conversation to bring about significant positive change in managing ADHD.

10.3. Case Study 3: Enhancing Teacher-Student Interactions

Tom, a high school Dance teacher, noticed behavioral problems with his student, Ryan, who had ADHD, resulting in clashes. Being advised by a colleague, Tom started implementing 'active listening', a communication tool that focuses on fully hearing and understanding the speaker's perspective.

In conversations with Ryan, Tom would repeat what he understood and ask Ryan to confirm or correct it. This method gave Ryan the feeling of being valued, establishing trust between him and Tom.

With the passage of time, Ryan's attitude towards Dance class improved significantly, demonstrating the benefits of effective student-teacher communication in managing ADHD symptoms.

10.4. Case Study 4: Enhancing Professional Relationships

Samantha, a project manager, faced difficulties managing Jason, a talented but usually distracted team member diagnosed with ADHD. Samantha realized conventional strategies weren't helping.

She then implemented a clear communication routine, ensuring that she provided Jason with detailed written instructions for each assignment. She also enforced regular check-ins for clarity and addressed Jason's questions patiently.

Gradually, Jason's productivity saw a marked improvement and so did the overall project timeline, reflecting how direct, straightforward communication can lead to considerable improvements in the workplace for individuals with ADHD.

10.5. Case Study 5: Self-Understanding and Self-Regulation

Michael, a university student with ADHD, constantly felt overwhelmed with his academic responsibilities, leading to heightened stress levels.

He decided to seek assistance from a psychotherapist, who introduced him to the concept of self-talk—a form of interior dialogue used als self-regulation tool. He was advised to use self-talk as a compass to navigate through challenging situations, helping him stay focused.

Being more mindful of his internal dialogue helped Michael manage his ADHD symptoms better, excel in his coursework, and decrease his overall stress level. This development further bolstered the premise that communication is not only about interaction with others, but also how effectively we converse with ourselves.

These real-life stories confirm how simple adjustments in the way we communicate can create profound changes for those living with ADHD. However, it's worth noting that each individual's journey with ADHD is unique, and it might require various forms of therapeutic interventions alongside improved communication strategies. Nevertheless, better conversation surely represents a promising initiative on the path towards a healthy balance in life.

Chapter 11. Looking Forward: Creating a Positive Communication Environment

Creating an atmosphere that promotes positive communication is not a one-time setup but rather an ongoing project that requires constant dedication. It unfolds in multiple layers, each contributing to the larger goal of effective interaction.

11.1. The Art of Active Listening

Active listening is a cornerstone in setting up a positive communication environment. It involves remaining fully engaged and attentive to what is being said, thereby conveying the idea that the speaker's viewpoint is respected and valued. It's more than just aural comprehension, but also about comprehending nonverbal cues and emotions.

In context to ADHD, this becomes even more vital since individuals with this condition often struggle with focusing on conversations. The first step toward active listening is basic attentiveness. Keep your body language open and be sure to make appropriate eye contact.

Another handy method in the process of active listening is the use of reflective techniques such as paraphrasing. It's a constructive practice of repeating the speaker's message in your own words. This not only confirms your comprehension but also reinstates the speaker's importance, thus fostering clear communication.

11.2. Importance of Empathy

Understanding begins with empathy. Empathy refers to our ability to connect emotionally with others, to step out of our shoes and into theirs so to speak, to view the world from their perspective. It is not about agreeing with the other person's point of view but merely acknowledging it.

For people with ADHD, empathy plays a big role in creating a positive environment. Empathy can help them feel comfortable sharing their feelings and thoughts without the fear of judgment. It also can establish a strong foundation of trust and mutual respect, essential ingredients in cultivating a fruitful communication climate.

11.3. Constructive Feedback and ADHD

When receiving feedback, individuals with ADHD can often feel overwhelmed, largely due to their heightened sensitivity. Therefore, it becomes crucial to give constructive feedback in a manner that is helpful rather than hurtful.

Start by offering a sincere acknowledgment of their efforts. Then, adopt a sandwich technique - placing the negative (constructive criticism) between the positives (appreciation). This method makes it easier for the recipient to accept criticism and understand the areas they need to improve.

Remember, the goal of feedback should always be improvement and growth, not blame or disparagement. It's crucial to direct the feedback towards the behavior or a specific event, rather than the person.

11.4. Creating a Safe Space for Open Dialogue

People with ADHD can often feel misunderstood, hence it's crucial to establish a safe space for open dialogue. Here, individuals feel comfortable expressing themselves without the fear of being dismissed or judged. It's about acknowledging their integral worth and unique experiences.

To create this, establish guidelines that include equal speaking time, respect for personal anecdotes, no interruption policy, etc. Reinforce the joint aim of problem-solving, instead of indulging in a blame game. This will foster a sense of equality, and people with ADHD will feel more comfortable and willing to participate in conversations.

11.5. Encouraging Self-Expression

Encouraging self-expression is another vital aspect. ADHD individuals often have trouble articulating their thoughts and feelings. Encouraging them to express themselves through varied mediums like drawing, writing, or even storytelling can be beneficial. These methods eschew the conventional dialogic pattern, coming across as less formidable, thereby making interaction more attainable and comfortable for them.

11.6. Emphasizing on Patience and Persistence

Change is not an overnight event but a gradual process. This observation aligns perfectly with developing a positive communication environment. One must continually focus on patience, understanding that people with ADHD may require more time to process and respond.

Persistence is also essential. Stumbles are natural in any growing process, and such a journey would involve a fair share of setbacks. However, perseverance is the key to overcoming these hurdles.

In conclusion, generating a positive communication environment for individuals with ADHD is a collective responsibility and shared journey. It caters not only to the immediate objective of facilitating conversation but goes beyond, aiming to bolster relationships and bolster self-confidence in these individuals, which will aid in their overall growth and development.